Simply Awesome Trips
Itineraries Ready To Go!

www.simplyawesometrips.com

Simply Awesome Trips offers personally experienced, detailed family trip itineraries to cities and outdoor destinations in the U.S. and abroad. Our goal is to help simplify your trip planning by sharing all the details you need for an enjoyable family vacation.

Each itinerary offers favorite lodging (including airbnb and VRBO), local food recommendations, activities that were fun for both kids and adults, labeled maps, rainy day activities, and any helpful trip tips discovered along the way--all organized into detailed, day-by-day plans.

We've put in the hours to research a fantastic trip, families have loved them, and we provide all you need to experience the same. You can duplicate the trip in its entirety or gather ideas for your own itinerary. Have fun, be safe, and enjoy your time in Amsterdam!

To see more trip destinations, visit our web page: www.simplyawesometrips.com

Happy Trails!

Amy & Amanda

Simply Awesome Trips
Itineraries Ready To Go!

Amsterdam
6 night Itinerary

Overview

Amsterdam, the Netherland's capital, is a lovely and charming city full of colorful architecture, canals and bridges, street markets, and world-class museums.

For families visiting from the United States, it's an easy introduction to visiting a European city as many residents speak

English and most museums and restaurants include written English along with Dutch.

You'll find plenty to do here between strolling alongside the canals, stopping at sidewalk cafes, eating Dutch delicacies, and exploring museums. It's a great family destination with something for everyone.

UNESCO World Heritage Site

Amsterdam's Canal Ring is unique in the world for its urban development and architectural artwork, as well as the physical expression of the major economic, political and cultural growth of the city in the Golden Age. The recognition of the uniqueness of the Canal Ring not only generates international attention for the city, it also frames a promise to maintain the area. In this way, everyone can continue to enjoy the unique living and working conditions of the Canal Ring. --www.IAmsterdam.com

It's a great city to roam and meander. It's a photographer's dream-- you would not be short-changed by this city if all you did during your entire trip was walk along the beautiful canals marveling at the charming architecture and canals.

Day	Activity
1	Welcome to Amsterdam! Check-in to your lodging, enjoy a canal-side stroll to the Bloemenmarkt and grab some groceries.
2 **(Best for a Monday)**	Eat traditional dutch pancakes, visit Anne Frank's house and Westerkerk (church), sample cheese at the Cheese Museum, stroll the nearby Jordaan neighborhood and finish off with Winkle 43's famous apple pie. (**If it's a Monday, include a visit to the Westerstraat Market and Noordermarkt held from 9am-1pm.)
3	Visit the Royal Palace, Dam Square, and stroll Kalverstratt to window shop and sample tasty goodies
4 **(Best for a sunny day)**	Get your Holland fix of windmills, wooden clogs, and cheese on this day trip to Zaanse-Schans.
5 **(Best for a weekday)**	Enjoy selfie-time at the I Amsterdam sign, go on a treasure hunt at the Van Gogh Museum, stroll one of the longest street markets in Europe, explore the playgrounds and cafes at the serene Vondelpark, and relax on a canal cruise.

Day	Activity
6	Have fun at the Nemo Science Museum. If you still have the energy, stop at the nearby National Maritime Museum.
7	Return home with great memories!

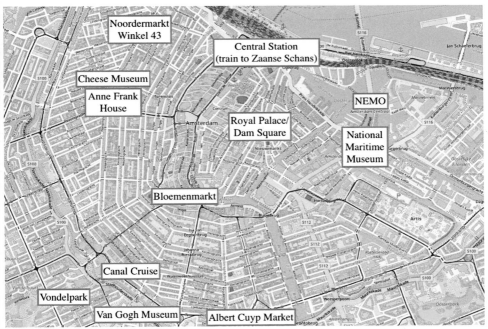

General Overview   Map courtesy of openstreetmaps.org

A Coffee Shop Is Not a "Coffee Shop"

An important note to understand about Amsterdam is that the term "Coffee Shop" refers to a business selling marijuana not coffee. Coffee shops are prevalent in all parts of the city, and you will smell their aroma walking by. It does not contribute a "seedy" flair to the city, and it went largely unnoticed by our kiddos.

As far as the Red Light District goes, you can easily avoid it. It's located northeast of the the Dam Square area, and it's a confined neighborhood. The De Oude Kerk is a famous landmark in the Red Light District and is easy to spot on most maps. For our walks, we never had to detour around it but it would be easy to do if needed.

I Amsterdam City Card

To purchase or not? We did not. Because children are admitted for free to many museums, the Iamsterdam City Card doesn't provide a family with additional savings unless you plan on visiting a multitude of museums.

4-day City Cards for a family of four costs € 392. They do not offer a special price for cards for children. Therefore, you must pay per person at 98 euro each (98x4=392).

Ticket prices for our family of four to attend the activities in this itinerary including Anne Frank House and the optional Maritime Museum cost €230.5. Adding Rijksmuseum tickets to this total would equal € 265.5, still less than purchasing 4 City Cards. See chart below.

Activities In Found In This Itinerary	Adult Ticket Price	Child Ticket Price	Price With IAmsterdam City Card	Family of 4 Total Cost without card
Canal Cruise	€16	€ 10 for 4 and older	Free	Family Price is € 44, 50
NEMO	€16	€16	Free	€64
Windmills at Zaanse Schans	€4	€2	Free	€12
Van Gogh	€18	free	Free	€36
Anne Frank	€9	€4,50	Not covered	€27
Unlimited access to Amsterdam's public transport system for 24, 48, 72 or 96 hours			Free	0- Didn't need to use trams
Maritime Museum (optional activity- included in total)	€16	€7.5	Free	€47
Rijksmuseum (optional activity--did not include in my total)	€17,50	free	Free	€35
Total Cost Without Card				€230.5

Activities In Found In This Itinerary	Adult Ticket Price	Child Ticket Price	Price With IAmsterdam City Card	Family of 4 Total Cost without card
City Card Cost	24 hrs € 59.00	48 hrs € 74.00	72 hrs € 87.00	96 hrs € 98.00 x 4= **€ 392**

Remember to slow down and enjoy the city as it is. You'll get a better feel if you limit your museums and enjoy the city walks along the canals and markets. For more info, visit their webpage to see a full list of sites and attractions covered by the IAmsterdam City Card.

https://www.iamsterdam.com/en/i-am/i-amsterdam-city-card

Arriving

You'll arrive in Schipol Airport, which is roughly a 20-30 minutes drive from city center. After an overseas flight, make it easy and take a taxi or Uber to avoid the hassle of the train with luggage and family in tow. Taxis will pick you up curbside at the airport with a charge of approximately € 40. Uber is a bit less expensive (around € 26) depending on the time of day.

If so inclined, you can catch a train from the airport to Central Station and then walk at least 15 minutes or take a tram / taxi / Uber to your final destination. One way train ticket is roughly € 6 each.

Transportation

Amsterdam is a very walkable city. Just be sure to be super aware of bikers, scooters, trams, and the occasional car. You have a higher chance of getting hit by a bike, just by the sheer number of them, so pay particular attention to bike lanes.

Tram lines run throughout the city, but all of the destinations in this itinerary are within a 30 minute walk of city central. We found it was faster to walk than take the trams.

Use the Ulmon City Maps2Go App to compare walking, tram, and Uber times to your destination. http://www.ulmon.com/The free app offers one offline city map of your choice.

Where To Stay

Amsterdam lodging is expensive. That being said, you can find beautiful canal-side apartments for almost the same price as sharing a hotel family room. If you can afford it, avoid the tourists and hustle and bustle found in city center near Dam Square and stay in the Western Canal Belt near the "Nine Streets" or Jordaan neighborhoods.

Generally speaking, it's the area comprising these three canals: Prinsengracht, Keizersgracht, and Herengracht, bordered on the north by Brouwersgracht and the south by Leidsegracht.

You'll have a quiet, village-like experience and will remain close to restaurants, attractions, and within a 30 minute walk of most sites and attractions. If you're within a 15 minute walk of Anne Frank House, it's a quiet location.

I've listed where we stayed as well as other places I considered. Determine your budget and you'll find plenty of options in this area. The listings below range from $2000-$3500 USD per week.

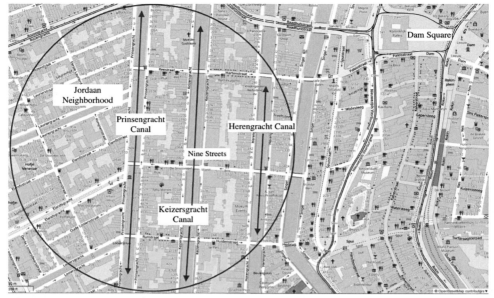

The Western Canal Belt Area is the best area to stay in Amsterdam

Recommended Lodging

The Canal View Apartment. We stayed in this spacious 2 bedroom canal front apartment located at 337 Keizersgracht. We loved the cozy 2 floor apartment with plenty of space and a terrific location, walkable to everything. Although it's located on a quiet street, it's next door to a wine bar that's open on weekend nights. We heard quite a bit of noise in our bedroom, but our girls didn't notice in the downstairs bedroom. Even with some noise, I loved this apartment.

Request an additional mattress for the 2nd bedroom as the bed is a small double. Also, please take note that the owner requires payment in cash. I made arrangements at home to get the Euro and brought it with me.

This is my review on booking.com:

"The apartment itself is fantastic if you can live with a bit of noise (not uncommon in a city)"

The wine bar next door played loud music during the weekend which we could hear from the upstairs bedroom but was relatively quiet downstairs. Ongoing construction noise in the mornings next door which is a temporary inconvenience. I wish that I had received an email with arrival instructions at least a few weeks before my trip. Communication with owner could have been better prior to visit but was fine upon arrival. Also, the cash only policy was a bit tedious.

Great space, clean and cozy, excellent storage, hot water and large shower, comfy beds, location, quiet street, views. Loved the market just down the street for takeaway food (2 minute walk). We walked everywhere from the apartment (Anne Frank, NEMO, Canal Cruise, Central Station, Van Gogh, etc. Be aware of steep stairs if you have children younger than 6. An extra mattress was set up in the downstairs bedroom which worked very well for our daughters. Each had her own bed but shared the room. Nice host met us at the apartment upon arrival. Would stay here again.
Stayed in March 2018

Upstairs living area

View from window

Cityden 2 Bedroom Apartment with Canal View. Canal Area. The location of this apartment is fantastic. They also offer a 3 bedroom in the same building.
http://cityden.com/pick-your-den/?type=cityden-canal

Cityden Jordan-9 Streets Serviced Apartment. 2 Bedroom Apartment. This apartment is also managed by Cityden and gets great reviews.
http://cityden.com/pick-your-den/?type=cityden-jordan-9-streets

Cityden Jordaan Canal. This would be my third choice in terms of the location of the apartments they offer.
http://cityden.com/pick-your-den/?type=jordan-canal

The Amsterdam Wiechman Hotel. Family Suite with canal view or a Quadruple Room. Located at Prinsengracht 328-332. Reserve through booking.com.

Jordaan Laurier Apartments. Offers 1 bedroom apartment that sleeps 4 with double bed and sofa bed as well as a 3 bedroom apartment. Located on Laurierstraat. Reserve through booking.com.

Day 1

Overview

Welcome to Amsterdam! Arrive and (hopefully), check-in to your apartment or hotel. Grab a bite to eat, take a 30 minute cat nap if needed, and explore your neighborhood. If you'd like a destination for your walk, stroll along the canals to reach the Bloemenmarkt (flower market) or find the famous bench from the movie/book "The Fault in Our Stars."

Walk to Bloemenmarkt (The Flower Market)

The walk to the Bloemenmarkt will take you along the city's canals to the world's only floating flower market. It's a good destination stroll to the city's southern canal belt.

You'll find flowers in bloom (in season: mid-March to mid-May) and tulip bulbs that you can purchase as souvenirs. Just make sure that they are "Certified" for travel to the U.S. If you're pressed for time on your return flight to the U.S., skip the tulip bulb purchase as it requires an additional line through Customs Agriculture.

Backside of the Bloemenmarkt located on Singel Canal

Bloemenmarkt

Fault in Our Stars

If you've read the book by John Greene (and many kids and adults have), you know that the later part of the book is set in Amsterdam and several scenes from the movie were filmed in Amsterdam. You can visit many of the sites from the movie if you'd like "direction" for your city strolling.

Seeing the infamous bench was on my daughter's list, so we made a point of walking by it on our walk.

It's located near the intersection of two Amsterdam canals, the Herengracht and Leidsegracht. You'll find it in front of the address Leidsegracht 2 and 4. For those not in the know, the bench looks like an ordinary green canal-side bench, but for fans of the book it apparently has meaning.

Other Fault in Our Stars Film Locations in Amsterdam
https://www.eatingamsterdamtours.com/blog/fault-in-our-stars-film-locations/

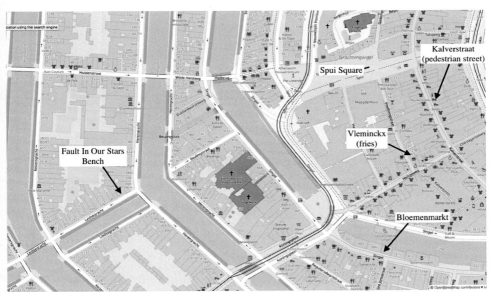

Map Courtesy of Openstreetmaps.org

Grocery Stores

On your way home, stop by the Marqt or Albert Heijn Grocery to stock up on supplies. You'll see these stores throughout Amsterdam. You'll be amazed by the quality and price of fine breads, cheese, delicious salads, chocolates, and wine. Stock up on whatever meets your fancy and consider takeout for dinner at your apartment. Purchase a package of stroopwafels for about € 2 for a tasty Dutch dessert.

Tip: Bring a soft-sided reusable grocery bag from home and take it with you each day so you can easily load up on goodies on the way back to your lodging. Unlike the U.S., you must provide your own grocery bag.

Albert Heijn
Important: Please note that not all Albert Heijn grocery stores accept credit card. We found that the one on Singel did accept cards while the one on Elandsgrach did not.

The Marqt
The Marqt offers takeout salads, pizza, cheese, chocolates, and a small bakery as well as regular grocery fare. It's a lot like a Whole Foods in the U.S., so it's a bit pricier than Albert Heijn and smaller (which I liked). It takes credit card only. **Tip:** The wine selection was better at Albert Heijns.
Wolvenstraat 32, 1016 EP Amsterdam, Netherlands
http://www.marqt.com

Day 2
(Make this a Monday or Saturday if you can)

Overview

Today, you'll explore the Jordaan and Westerpark neighborhoods to visit the Anne Frank House and hopefully attend one of the Monday or Saturday street markets. After the somberness of Anne Frank, you'll enjoy the emotional and gastronomical pick-me-up of the Amsterdam Cheese Museum.

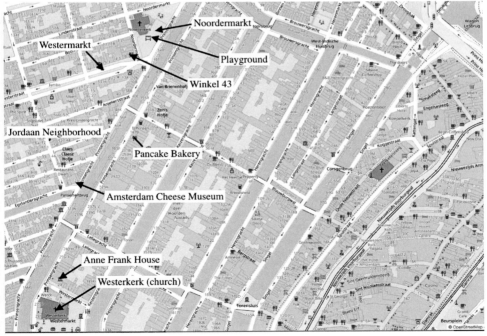

Map Courtesy of Openstreetmaps.org

Day 1 Morning-Breakfast at Pancakes!

If you didn't eat at your lodging, grab breakfast at **Pancakes!**
Located at Berenstraat 38 and opens at 9am. They serve traditional
Dutch pancakes as well as American-style pancakes in case you
have picky eaters. It's a pricey breakfast with most entrees ranging
from € 8-11. The **Pancake Bakery** also makes the cut for excellent
food and is located nearby the Anne Frank House.

The Marqt is nearby for a less expensive option. We like their
croissants.

https://pancakes.amsterdam/locations/1/pancakes-amsterdam-negen-straatjes

The Dutch take their pancakes seriously. Here's a breakdown of
their favorite pancakes houses in Amsterdam.

https://amsterdam-mamas.nl/articles/our-10-favorite-pancake-eateries-amsterdam

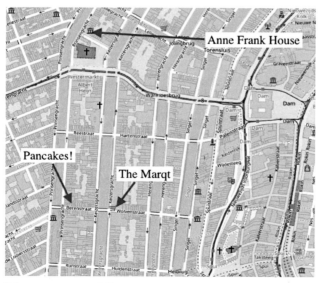

Map courtesy of Openstreetmaps.org

Westermarket and Noordermarket (Mondays and Saturdays)

If you're fortunate enough to be here on a Monday or Saturday, you can walk through the Westermarket and Noordermarket held from 9-1pm. A market stroll is one of the best ways to see the locals, sample foods, and buy souvenirs to bring home.

The Westermarket runs the length of Westerstraat, and Noordermarket is clustered around the church near Winkel 43, a cafe famous for their apple pie. You can easily visit both on your walk as they intersect each other at Prinsengracht.

The Monday market focuses more on fabrics, purses, hats, clothing, and more. You'll find a larger selection of food on Saturdays. We found the Noordermarket to have a fun shopping selection of Amsterdam t-shirts and discounted fashion items like shoes, purses, etc. as well as some food options.

Westermarket

Jordaan Stroll

If you have time, the Jordaan neighborhood is a peaceful stroll. Some of the more quaint streets include Tweede Tuindwarsstraat, Tweede Egelantiersdwarsstraat, and Tweede Anjeliersdwarsstraat. All within a 5 minute walk from the Anne Frank House and Noordermarkt.

Some advice from the Just Go Places Blog:
Go hunting for stone tablets that grace the buildings of the Jordaan. In the old days, these tablets would indicate the profession of the people inside. In the 16th century, these tablets were used as signs instead of wooden gables that blocked the little streets.
http://www.justgoplacesblog.com/16-things-to-do-in-the-trendy-jordaan-with-children/

Anne Frank House

One of Amsterdam's most popular and important museums is the Anne Frank House. The house is located on the Prinsengracht canal in the centre of Amsterdam. It contains the secret annex where the young Anne Frank and seven others hid from German occupation during WW2. It was here that she wrote her now famous diary.

Before your visit to Amsterdam, consider reading part if not all of Anne Frank's Diary. Or, read the children's book, "Who Is Anne Frank?" It will make the tour of the house more meaningful and provide a historical context. The house is located at 267 Prinsengracht.

Important: Make reservations online in advance. Tickets are available 2 months in advance. € 9 adults, € 4.50 ages 10-17, free under 9 years of age.
http://www.annefrank.org/

Visiting With Children- The Museum's website offers a nice article about visiting the museum with children. The Museum recommends that children be 10 years and older, but I found it suitable for my 7 year-old. We did, however, skip the first film which contains images of concentration camps that might be shocking. You could prepare your child for this, or decide to skip the film.

We found it to be a very worthwhile visit, and my girls appreciated seeing the space and imagining what the Frank's life must have been like during that time. It really made history come alive for them.

Tip: If you arrive early, you can enter the 17th century Westerkerk (church) next to the Anne Frank House. Anne points out the sound of its church bell in her diary, and Rembrandt's body is presumed to be buried in it. It's free to enter. Westerkerk is open to visitors all year round from 10am-3pm, except during Sunday services.

Westerkerk church in the distance. Photo taken from the outside of the Amsterdam Tulip Museum next door the Cheese Museum.

Amsterdam Cheese Museum

You will absolutely love this stop. In this "museum", you will be able to sample all types of cheese and purchase any that you like. Free admission, free cheese, score! It's a great way to determine what you like to help you navigate the beautiful cheese selection at the Marqt and Albert Heijns.

In the downstairs, you'll find the small "museum" which chronicles the history and art of cheesemaking but most importantly offers a free camera shoot complete with Dutch costumes and props such as bonnets, cheese heads, pitch forks, and more. We had a blast. You can have your image emailed to you for a keepsake.

It's a 2 minute walk from the Anne Frank House and is located at Prinsengracht 112.
http://www.cheesemuseumamsterdam.com/ (9am-7pm)

The downstairs of the Amsterdam Cheese Museum

Restaurants Near the Anne Frank Museum and Jordaan Neighborhood

Winkel 43

Try the Apple Pie at Winkel 43. A Dutch culinary fixture located at the corner of Prinsengracht and Westerstraat. It's right next to the Noorderkerk (church) and about a 7 minute walk from the Anne Frank house. The remarkable thing about it is that everyone orders the apple pie and coffee but I didn't even see it on the menu. Weird!
http://www.winkel43.nl/

Winkel 43

Tastes as good as it looks!

Pancakes Amsterdam

Another pancake house near Anne Frank House--277 Prinsengracht
https://pancakes.amsterdam/

La Perla Pizzeria

Wood-fired pizzas, pasta and salads with outdoor seating. Tweede Tuindwarsstraat 53
http://pizzaperla.nl/

Cafe Thijssen

This attractive cafe with large outdoor dining looked affordable and fun. Brouwersgracht 107 http://cafethijssen.nl/

Neighborhood Playgrounds

Noorderkerk Playground

When not hosting the Monday or Saturday Noordermarket, the plaza outside of the Noorderkerk church has a small playground. A good place to get the wiggles out before eating apple pie at the nearby Winkle 43.

Noorderkerk Playground

Kip and Konintje (Chicken and Bunny) Playground

If you have young children, you might seek out the Kip and Konintje (Chicken and bunny) playground at the end of Slootstraat off of Madelievenstraat. As the name implies, you'll find a small house with chickens and bunnies for the kids to admire along with swings, a small slide and a sandpit. It's about a 7 minute walk from the Anne Frank House.

http://www.konippen.nl/

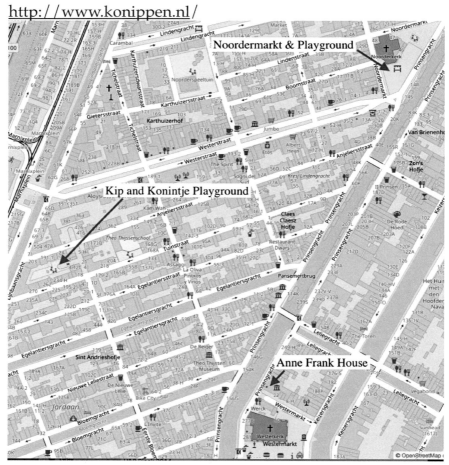

Map courtesy of Openstreetmaps.org

Day 3

Overview

Today is a built-in light day to visit the Royal Palace and explore Dam Square. You'll also walk down the nearby touristy, pedestrian shopping street Kalverstraat for window shopping and have some amazing treats.

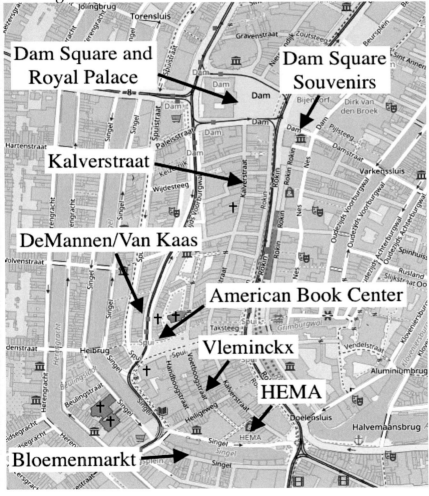

Map courtesy of Openstreetmaps.org

Dam Square and the Royal Palace

Royal Palace Tour

Located in the heart of the city, the magnificent 17th century Royal Palace is not only one of the Netherlands' most famous historical buildings, it is the only palace in the country that is both in active use and available for the public to visit.

You'll be in awe at its history, beauty, the artwork, sculptures, furniture, and extravagant chandeliers. Better yet, they offer a scavenger hunt for the kids, free audio guides, and a cloak room to store your bags and coats at no charge.

Plan about an hour to explore. Open 10-5pm; € 10 adults, kids free.

https://www.paleisamsterdam.nl/en/

10 Things to Know About the Princess

A fun note for your kiddos: Princess Catharina-Amalia, 14, the oldest child of King Willem-Alexander and Queen Maxima, is first in line to the throne. She is followed by her sisters Alexia and Ariane. Under a 1983 law, the eldest son <u>or</u> daughter becomes heir whereas historically it has been the eldest son.
<u>https://us.hellomagazine.com/royalty/2014120722316/princess-catharina-amalia-birthday-new-photos/</u>

Dam Square Souvenirs

Stop by this souvenir store for yet another photo op in a giant, yellow Dutch shoe with Dam Square as a backdrop. It's also a nice souvenir shop with reasonable prices. We purchased a windmill Christmas ornament and some fun clog pencil holders.

Simply Awesome Tip: Print out a 10% off coupon on the website. Address: Dam 17-19. <u>http://dutchsouvenirs.com</u>/

Outside Dam Souvenirs

Stroll Kalverstraat and Window Shop

The pedestrian-only street Kalverstratt stretches from Dam Square to the Bloemenmarkt and is filled with main stream fashion stores, department stores, souvenir shops, cafes, and more. Lots of people and lots of tourists. It can be crowded but is worth a stroll if you have brand-obsessed pre-teens. Factoid: Kalverstraat is the most expensive street in the Dutch version of the Monopoly game.

Vleminckx

After about a 10 minute stroll, it's time to experience the best fries in Amsterdam at Vleminckx. Walking on Kalverstraat from the Dam, turn right on Heiligeweg and then take another right at the Le Creuset store to proceed on Voetboogstraat. You'll see the small storefront (and the waiting line) on the right. Voetboogstraat 33.

Determine your serving size and sauce and enjoy. Mayonnaise is the the traditional Dutch sauce. Or, try the herby ketchup, which does not taste quite like Heinz. The satay sauce was different and good too. The fries are served in paper cones with a small wooden fork to dig up the saucy remnants. **Tip**: The restaurant across the street will allow you to bring in your fries if you order a drink. http://vleminckxdesausmeester.nl/en/

Amsterdam Wonderland offers a great description and menu. https://amsterdamwonderland.com/2016/06/15/best-chips-in-amsterdam/

Hema Department Store

Back on Kalverstraat, you could continue your unhealthy food binge at HEMA Department Store's street-front snack shop to get the best ice cream deal in the city: a soft-serve cone with your choice of sprinkles for € 1.25.

If you feel inclined, you can take the escalator down to the department store for a Target-like shopping experience. Department stores in other countries are always interesting, and we generally make a point to walk through them to see the different products they offer. This one offered a nice selection of affordable stationary, kitchen gadgets, clothing, and food products.

Otherwise, keep walking. Kalvertoren shopping mall. Kalverstraat 212

American Book Center

If you enjoy a good bookstore, this one's for you. Located in the Spui neighborhood, you can also find an outdoor book market nearby on Fridays. The books are pricey considering the exchange rate, but you'll find an amazing selection. The travel selection alone was incredible. Spui 12 https://www.abc.nl/

Book Market in Spui Square- Fridays 10-6pm.
https://www.amsterdam.info/markets/bookmarket/

Nearby Restaurants

Vleminckx
Best fries in Amsterdam. http://vleminckxdesausmeester.nl/en/

DeMannen/Van Kaas
Our favorite food find. If we were anywhere in the vicinity of this fine food shop, we would stop in for cheese samples and sandwiches to go. Crazy good. Spuistraat 330.
http://www.demannenvankaas.nl/

The incredible sandwiches from DeMannen/Van Kaas

Bierfabriek

Brewery and food near Spui. Opens at 3pm weekdays; 1pm weekends

https://www.bierfabriek.com/amsterdam/en/menu-2/

Kantijil en de Tiger

This restaurant was recommended to us for its good rijsttafel. *Rijsttafel* (translation: "rice table"), pronounced RICE-taffle, is a medley of dishes from the Indonesian islands. You will see plenty of Indonesian restaurants in Amsterdam as Indonesia was a Dutch colony for more than 350 years. It was a fun dinner and a nice place. We shared a rijstfafel (with a set selection of dishes) for 2 among the 4 of us for about € 32. Lunch: 12:00 - 16:30; Dinner: 16:30 - 23:00. Spuistraat 291.

https://www.kantjil.nl/en/lunch/lunch-menu

Le Pain Quotidien

Bakery, soups, sands, baguettes. Same chain as found in the U.S. Spuistraat 266

http://www.lepainquotidien.nl/en/store/english-spuistraat/

Stach Food

Sandwiches (brooj) and burgers to go, pastries, 8:30am-10pm. Singel 437.

http://www.stach-food.nl

Het Pakhuis

Cozy Dutch cafe on a hidden side street off Spui has a reasonable lunch-time menu.

https://eetcafehetpakhuis.nl/en/

Day 4

Day Trip to Zaanse Schans

Located just north of Amsterdam, the Zaanse Schans offers a perfectly preserved glimpse into the Netherlands' industrial past with its traditional houses, windmills, warehouses and workshops.

In its 18th and 19th century heyday, the Zaan region was an important industrial area dotted by hundreds of windmills producing linseed oil, paint, snuff, mustard, paper and other products. Many of the Zaanse Schans' characteristic village houses are now museums, gift shops or workshops while others are still used as private residences. Some of the Zaanse Schans' remaining windmills are also open to the public.--www. IAmsterdam.com

If you're traveling to Holland, you need to see windmills, and this is the place to do it. It's a great way to spend a lazy day admiring the view while strolling the grounds filled with cheese shops, clog workshops, and more. It's especially beautiful when the weather is nice. A visit to the village of Zaanse Schans is free, but some sites require an admission fee. For instance, each windmill has an admission of €3-4 to climb up to an observation deck.

It's located 30 minutes from Amsterdam by train which includes a 10-15 minute walk from the Koog-Zaandijk station. Or, it's a 40 minute bus ride from Central Station.

Plan on strolling the grounds, taking a zillion photos of the windmills, sampling cheese, touring the clog museum, and visiting the spice windmill, all for free. Skip the Zaanse Schans card which offers discounted entry to certain windmills and the Zaans Museum which focuses on the food industry of Holland.

You'll have a great time just strolling through the village and walking by the windmills. Make sure to visit these free attractions:

- **The Clog Workshop** with its live demonstrations and scenic photo op in yet another giant Dutch shoe.

- **The Cheese Shop** for free samples and a visit with the farm animals behind it

- **The Spice Windmill** (Specerijenmagazijn) which has free admittance inside (though no viewing platform) and smells divine.

View from the bridge

Zaanse Schans is highly recommended though it is a very touristy spot. Visiting in March minimized the crowds significantly, but I imagine it is super, perhaps crazy busy in the summer. https://www.dezaanseschans.nl/en/

You can also rent bikes in season and bike an 8 km or 30 km ride on the bike paths surrounding the village: https://www.dezaanseschans.nl/en/discover/bike-rental-and-cycling-routes/

Or take a boat tour: https://www.dezaanseschans.nl/en/discover/boat-tour/

Getting There By Bus
Take bus 391 from the back of Amsterdam Central Station Platform E which leaves every 15 minutes and takes about 40 minutes. A single ticket is €5 (€1 for under 11-year olds). Buy from the driver. Zaanse Schans is the last stop before the bus turns around and returns to Amsterdam. For more information: www.bus391.nl.

Getting There By Train
The nearest railway station is called either Zaandijk–Zaanse Schans or Koog-Zaandijk. You can purchase a ticket to either destination, it's the same. This station can be reached by local train from Amsterdam Central Station in 17 minutes with a total of 4 stops. Subsequently walk to the Zaanse Schans in 15 minutes.

It's a beautiful walk from the station with the smell of chocolate in the air from the nearby cocoa factory. You will also pass a wonderful bakery if you're hungry for a snack. Crossing the bridge over the Zaans River with an incredible view of the windmills

further ahead was a highlight. The path is clearly marked with signs, and you'll have no trouble finding it.

You'll pay more for the train than the bus. We paid € 24 roundtrip for the 4 of us on the train, however my daughter really wanted to ride in a train and we avoided some apprehension about motion sickness.

Tip: Make sure you call your credit card company to acquire a pin number to use your credit card at the automated train ticket machines in Central Station. Otherwise, you will have to wait in line to buy a ticket.

Use This Excellent Detailed Step-By-Step Guide for Arriving By Train
http://mikestravelguide.com/the-easiest-way-to-get-from-amsterdam-central-station-to-zaanse-schans/
A good blog post on Zaanse-Schans:
http://travelwithbender.com/travel-blog/netherlands/zaanse-schans-best-place-see-windmills-holland

Nearby Restaurants

The village itself offers a Pancake House and restaurant. https://www.dezaanseschans.nl/en/discover/hospitality/

If you can't wait, stop at the bakery **De Wijn.** This bakery is located on the walk from the station to Zaanse-Schans. One of the best sandwiches we had in Holland. The girls enjoyed their croissants. 8am-5pm Monday-Friday; 8-4pm Saturday; closed on Sundays. Stationsstraat 7. https://www.banketbakkerijdewijn.nl/

Day 5

Overview

Today, you'll start with an early morning photo shoot at the iconic IAmsterdam Sign before touring the Van Gogh Museum. Afterwards, head to Albert Cuyp Market to eat and souvenir shop. Finally, wrap up the day at the playgrounds in Vondelpark and rest your feet on a Canal Cruise.

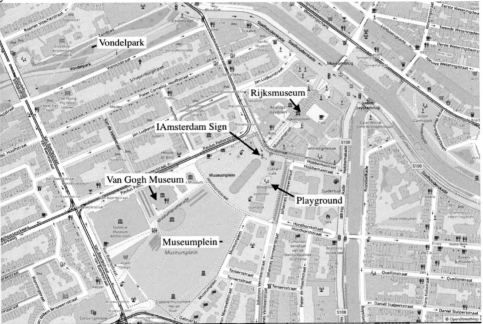

Map courtesy of openstreetmaps.org

I Am Amsterdam Sign

You'll have a great photo shoot at the infamous I Am Amsterdam Sign located right behind the Rijksmuseum. To find the sign, you'll walk through the pedestrian and biking tunnels of the Rijksmuseum to access Museumplein.

Walk through the tunnel to get to the I Am Amsterdan Sign and Museumplein

Tip: Get there early to avoid the crowds. If it's too crowded, go to the other side of the sign to take your photo. By taking the photo from the backside, you will avoid all the people and you can simply inverse the photo later on your computer. If you use Picasso for photo editing, click the image and use Control/Shift/H on your keyboard. Voila! For other photo editing programs, google "how to flip an image horizontally using _____"

Inverted photo where we have the sign all to ourselves

The other side with everyone else

Rijksmuseum

The Rijksmuseum is one of Amsterdam's grandest and most popular museums. Its vast collection showcases iconic art as well as Dutch and global history. You'll find Rembrandt's large-scale painting, *The Night Watch*, here along with other Dutch Masters. It's a larger museum, so we opted to visit the nearby smaller and more-manageable Van Gogh Museum. If you do decide to tackle this beauty, see this link for highlights. https://www.iamsterdam.com/en/see-and-do/things-to-do/museums-and-galleries/top-10-rijksmuseum-highlights

Van Gogh Museum

The Rijksmuseum and the Van Gogh Museum are two of the most famous art museums in Amsterdam. The larger Rijksmuseum focuses on Dutch art (Rembrandt and Vermeer are highlighted here) while the Van Gogh Museum holds the largest collection of Van Gogh paintings under one roof along with other Impressionist artists.

We found the Van Gogh Museum to be a perfect introduction for our kids. It takes about an hour to visit, and the museum provides a Treasure Hunt Worksheet (at no additional cost) for children aged 6 to 12. I recommend skipping the audio guide so you can go at your own pace.

Van Gogh Treasure Hunt

The kid's Treasure Hunt information can be found at the information desk one level above the coat check. You can check your coat and bag upon entry on the ground floor at no cost.

The Treasure Hunt was fun and informative, and we all enjoyed it (kids and adults). At the end of the tour, the kids get a prize for

completing the worksheet. Each child was treated with their choice of a postcard of a famous Van Gogh painting and a sticker.

Tip: Before leaving the museum, get your photo taken at the automated machine near the coat check for a fun souvenir. It will take your photo and email it to you for free.

Van Gogh Museum Tickets

Purchase tickets in advance online. You'll need to specify your date and time. Early times are always better to avoid the crowds. You can enter the museum up to 30 minutes after your reserved starting time. Purchasing your ticket online in advance means you benefit from priority access and won't have to visit the ticket office. Tickets are € 18 for adults and free for kids under age 18.
https://www.vangoghmuseum.nl/en

Museumplein

After touring the museum or before entering, soak in the beautiful views of Museumplein while the kiddos get their wiggles out at the playground near the I Am Amsterdam sign.

Museumplein

Albert Cuyp Market

With 260 stands, the Albert Cuyp Market is the largest day market in Europe. Stalls sell everything from fruit, vegetables, cheese, fish and spices to clothes, cosmetics, art, shoes, and luggage. And much, much, more. It's huge. It's a great place to buy Poffertjes and Stroopwafels as well as other hot dishes both ethnic and Dutch.

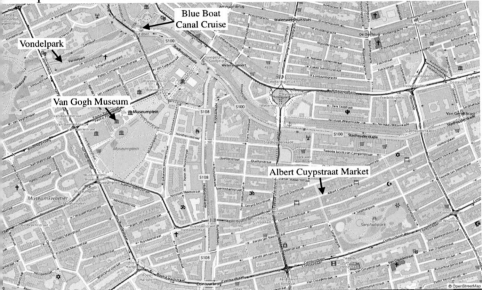

If you're brave enough, you can also try raw herring from one of the herring stands. It's apparently the best here at the market if you can summon yourself to partake of it.

Souvenirs

The souvenir prices are the best in town here. For instance, soccer jerseys were purchased for € 9 and the souvenir knick-knacks were the least expensive compared to other shops in the city. 9am-5; closed Sundays.

http://albertcuyp-markt.amsterdam/?lang=en

Albert Cuyp Market

Getting There

The market is a 15 minute walk (0.75 miles) from the Van Gogh Museum.

Tip: Go on a weekday if possible to avoid the weekend crowds.

Restaurants Nearby

The Butcher

If you didn't eat enough street food at the market, The Butcher offers one of the best flame-broiled burgers in town. You'll find it behind the market stalls at Albert Cuypstraat 129. Keep in mind that seating in The Butcher is limited and the place gets extremely busy on weekends. http://the-butcher.com/about.html

Vondelpark

After filling up at the market, walk back towards the Museum Area to visit Vondelpark. Vondelpark is Amsterdam's largest and most famous municipal park. Its tree-lined paths take you to numerous children's playgrounds, a wading pool, rose garden, and several cafés and restaurants. You can even see an original Picasso sculpture here.

Vondelpark Map
http://ontheworldmap.com/netherlands/city/amsterdam/vondelpark-map.jpg.

*When looking at the map, note that WC indicates toilets, yellow 7 circle is Cafe Groot Melkhuis and yellow circle 9 is the paddling pool (waterspeeltuin). Speeltuin (yellow 2 circle) means playground.

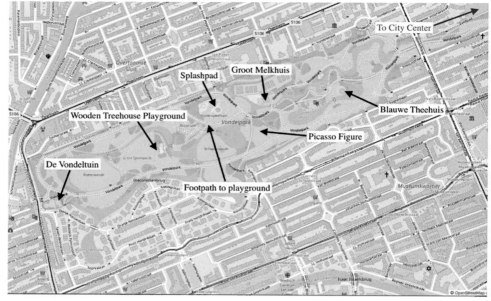

Map of Vondelpark

Fun Playground

Take a stroll to the wooden treehouse-like playground found near the center of the park. The kiddos enjoyed the enclosed bridges and forts. The entire walkway is enclosed with netting and ropes, so it's safe for younger kids as well.

To find this particular playground, locate the splash pools (waterspeeltuin). With it on your right walking south, take the footpath on your left. You'll eventually arrive at a white wooden bridge and it's straight ahead.

Follow this footpath
to reach the wooden playground

Small playground and splash pool.
Toilets nearby.

One of the playgrounds in Vondelpark

Best Description of Vondelpark and Its Playgrounds
https://babyccinokids.com/blog/2016/07/04/vondelpark/

Vondelpark Restaurants

Vondelpark has several cafes within the park. **The Groot Melkhuis** has a beautiful outdoor terrace and the children can play in their proprietary playground while you enjoy a beverage. Open 10-5, closed Mon. and Tues.
http://www.grootmelkhuis.nl/en/

The Groot Melkhuis

Blauwe Theehuis is another cafe in the park. It's architecture and ambiance is not nearly as attractive as Groot Melkhuis. 9-5 weekdays and 10-5 weekends
http://www.blauwetheehuis.nl/en/

De Vondeltuin is located at the southern end of the park, furthest from Amsterdam center, and looks like a nice place to grab a coffee or lunch. Pretty outdoor seating. Kids menu too. A good playground is nearby.
http://www.vondeltuin.nl

Canal Cruise

Now it's time to sit and enjoy the ride. There are many canal cruise operators, but we chose the Blue Boat Company for their location (just outside Vondelpark) and their "Pirate Cruise" option (no up charge) for kids aged 5-12. The kids get a pirate-themed audio guide, worksheet, and a pair of "binoculars." My 7 year-old daughter really enjoyed it, but I think my 11 year-old would have preferred the adult audio with the worksheet.

The boats have a restroom on board, and you can bring snacks and beverages either purchased at the ticket office or elsewhere.

The boats leave daily every half hour between 10:00 and 18:00. Lasts 75 minutes. A **Family Ticket** costs € 44.

Canal Boat Tips:

- Although the company does provide headphones for all, bring your child's headphones or earbuds for a better fit.

- The left side of the boat may have slightly better views but not significantly better if you can't sit there. If it's a nice day, you can sit in the open-air area at the rear of the boat but there's no audio plug-in.

- If you booked your lodging on booking.com, they often offer a discount code. Look for a discount found in an "Attractions in Amsterdam" email. Our price with **Booking.com**= € 9.95 and € 6,50 for kids.

Located near Vondelpark; across from Hard Rock Cafe; Look for blue umbrella. Corner of Stadhouderskade 30 1071 and Hobbenmastraat.

Summer season (March-October): Leaves daily every half hour from 10:00-18:00

Blue Boat Ticket office

Day 6

NEMO Museum

If you have a bad weather day, this would be the place to go. But even on a good weather day, it's worth the visit. The science museum designed for kids resides in a large green building shaped like a ship and spans 4 floors. Even better, its rooftop cafe and terrace offer a spectacular view of the city. From the terrace, you can also see "The Amsterdam", a ship housed at the National Maritime Museum.

It's a fantastic, interactive science museum that mixes the science behind each station with fun. My kids both had a blast. We originally planned a 2 hour excursion here, and it quickly turned into 4. It's super interactive and was fun for all ages, including adults.

Favorite stops included the gear pulleys, interactive mechanical arms, illusions, and the shadow capture. You can even touch a 1.2 billion year old rock or perform real laboratory experiments complete with white coat and safety glasses. All exhibits were in English and Dutch.

They provide lockers for your bags and coats. Deposit 50 cent euro in the coin slot of the locker to get the key and remember to get your coin back when you leave.

Note to Parents: Be forewarned that the 4th floor, "Humania", contains a Teen Area with an interactive "puppet french kissing" exhibition and a sex room with various poses rated xxx. Only in Amsterdam! Don't skip the 4th floor though. You can experience other activities like facial cue recognition, IQ tests, learning style, brain size, and more. The Teen Area is easily avoidable as it's located in the rear area of the floor, and you don't have to walk through it to see other exhibits.

Tip: Even if you don't buy tickets, you can go to the rooftop viewing area by climbing the steps on the eastern edge of the building or taking the elevator from the museum's central hall at the front. A great way to get an awesome view of the city.

Open 10am-5:30pm; Allow 2 hours or more. Entry costs € 16 for anyone over 4. You can also buy e-tickets online which are valid for one year after issue date.
https://www.nemosciencemuseum.nl/en/

Getting There
It's a 15-minute walk from Central Station. Leave the main entrance of Central Station, turn left and follow the signs for 'Route Oosterdok', walk by the Double Tree Hotel, and walk straight ahead to the pedestrian bridge leading to NEMO.

From the eastern part of the City Centre/Waterlooplein, follow the Valkenburgerstraat to NEMO pier.

Best Blog Post on NEMO: Amsterdam Wonderland
https://amsterdamwonderland.com/2016/06/14/nemo/

Nearby Restaurants

NEMO
You'll find a nice cafeteria style restaurant on the top floor (5th) of NEMO for a snack or lunch. Offers pizza slices, hot dogs, salads, and sandwiches. Not terribly expensive for the convenience. Or, you can bring your own.

Amsterdam's Central Library
Located next door to NEMO, it has a well-reviewed, inexpensive 7th floor cafe. Dining with a view. The library is apparently a beautiful example of what a children's library should be. It's open every day of the week from 10:00 to 22:00 hrs.

See Babyccino's blog for a nice description of the library: https://babyccinokids.com/blog/2016/11/24/amsterdam-central-library/?c=amsterdam-see

Nearby Sites
Two fun alternatives or additions to this day if you have endless energy would be the National Maritime Museum (Hetscheepvaartmuseum) or a side trip to a brewery, Brouwerij 't IJ, housed next to an old windmill.

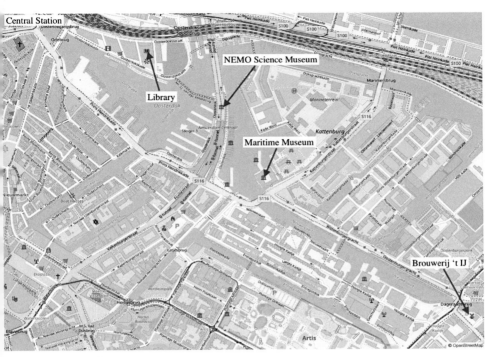

Map courtesy of openstreetmaps.org

National Maritime Museum

If I had another day, this would have been our next stop. A recently renovated, interactive museum geared to kids and adults. Per their website:

The National Maritime Museum invites visitors to discover how the sea has shaped Dutch culture. In this freshly modernised museum, stimulating, interactive exhibitions let visitors explore 500 years of maritime history. There are a variety of exhibitions, including many especially for children. Notably, the famous replica of the Dutch East India Company ship 'Amsterdam' is moored at the museum, so visitors can climb on board and explore it.

Open 9-5 Children 4 - 17 € 8,00 Adults 18 and up € 16,00

View of the Maritime Museum from NEMO

https://www.hetscheepvaartmuseum.nl/
https://www.amsterdam.info/museums/
netherlands_maritime_museum/

Brouwerij 't IJ

This brewery combines two things I love in Holland: beer and windmills. The brewery is located right next to the largest wooden windmill in the Netherlands making it the ideal landmark. Although this place is mainly about the beer, it also offers wine,

juice, and sodas along with a basic menu of beer snacks (cheeses, sausages, etc).

Brouwerij 't IJ

It's a bit off city center and not on the way to anywhere, so it's a destination that requires an additional 20 minute walk from NEMO or a 15 minute walk from the Maritime Museum. Uber might be the way to go here. Open 2pm-8pm every day. Address: Funenkade 7 1018 AL Amsterdam

http://www.brouwerijhetij.nl/?lang=en

Best Resources

Best Amsterdam Blog: https://amsterdamwonderland.com
Best Travel Guide: *Top 10 Amsterdam by Eye Witness*
Best Overall Website: IAmsterdam.com

Before Your Trip (Fun)

- Read Fault In Our Stars and watch the movie
- Watch Ocean's 12 (filmed in Amsterdam)
- Read the Diary of Anne Frank
- Read *Who Is Anne Frank?*
- Check out a book about Van Gogh's work from the library
- Purchase *Mission Amsterdam* from Amazon ($12.99). It provides a fun city-wide scavenger hunt for kids. My daughter really enjoyed it and most of the sites we visited were in it. https://www.amazon.com/Mission-Amsterdam-Scavenger-Adventure-Travel/dp/0989226700

Before Your Trip (Logistics)

- Call your credit card and bank to let them know you are traveling in Amsterdam
- Download Ulmon City Maps2Go App or download offline Google Map
- Make sure your Passport is up to date
- Call your cell phone provider to get international coverage. With AT&T, it costs $10 for each day we used cellular. Some days we only used WiFi and didn't pay a fee for that day.
- Download the Uber app if you don't already have it. We used it with no problem, plenty of drivers for our trip back to the airport.

If I Had More Time

You would think 6 days would be ample time to visit Amsterdam, but we left wanting more. Here are the other activities on our list for next time.

National Maritime Museum (located near Nemo)

https://www.hetscheepvaartmuseum.nl

Rijksmuseum

The Rijksmuseum is one of Amsterdam's grandest and most popular museums. Its vast collection showcases iconic art as well as Dutch and global history. You'll find Rembrandt's large-scale painting, *The Night Watch*, here along with other Dutch Masters.

https://www.rijksmuseum.nl/en

Amsterdam Museum

A visit to Amsterdam Museum might be worthwhile if you're interested in an historical overview. But if you're short on time, you can also take a walk through their free gallery and marvel at the bizarre gable stones hanging on the wall close to the entrance. Kalverstraat 92. Monday Opening Hours: 10 am – 5 pm

amsterdammuseum.nl

Foodhallen

Think super-extravaganza foodcourt for all foodies. Viet View for Vietnamese street food is recommended as well as Petit Gateau for dessert. Kanarie Club at the back for a drink. http://foodhallen.nl

Herring Stand at Albert Cuyp Market- we're going to try it!

IJ Kantine at NDSM Wharf

The IJ-Kantine prides itself on being a family-friendly restaurant, providing a children's menu and even a staff member leading craft activities on Sundays at 2pm. During the summer, a huge sandpit at the side of the terrace is supplied with toys. You will enjoy the nice outdoor terrace while the kiddos play. Everyone is happy.

Part of the fun is getting there. Take the free GVB ferry from behind Amsterdam Central Station to NDSM-werf. These run approximately every half hour to midnight- - last ferry back to central is 1am Fridays and Saturdays.

Brouwerij 't IJ

This brewery combines two things I love in Holland: beer and windmills. The brewery is located right next to the largest wooden windmill, De Gooyer windmill. http://www.brouwerijhetij.nl/?lang=en

The Cat Boat

The Catboat is the only animal sanctuary that literally floats. A refuge for stray and abandoned cats which, thanks to its unique location on a houseboat in Amsterdam's picturesque canal belt, has also become a world-famous tourist attraction. I think my girls would have gotten a kick out of this this. Singel 38. Open 1-3pm. https://depoezenboot.nl/en

Bike Along the Amstel River to Ouderkerk Aan de Amstel

Hire a bike in town and cycle the 10k along the Amstel River. Heading out past the Magere Brug or "Skinny Bridge" you'll be in the 'countryside' within about 20 minutes, cycling past windmills and fabulous waterfront properties before riding out on the polder with the Amstel snaking alongside you. Its not surprising that the easy 40 minute ride is one of the city's most popular out-of-town day trips for saddle-bound explorers.

https://amsterdamwonderland.com/2018/02/01/why-a-trip-to-ouderkerk-aan-de-amstel-is-a-must-for-a-taste-of-the-dutch-countryside-just-outside-the-city/

Free Lunchtime Concert at Het Concertgebouw
Per their website:

For many years now, free Lunchtime Concerts have been held in the Main Hall and the Recital Hall. Usually, these Lunchtime Concerts take place on Wednesdays, but please check the concert schedule as this occasionally changes. The concerts range from public rehearsals by the Royal Concertgebouw Orchestra, to chamber music performances by young up-and-coming artists.

The concerts last thirty minutes and are free of charge. For Lunchtime Concerts in the Recital Hall you will require a ticket, which is free of charge. These tickets are available from the Entrance Hall, from 11:30 a.m. onwards. As these concerts are very popular, please ensure you arrive in time to obtain your ticket. Doors to the concert hall open about 30 minutes before the Lunchtime Concert starts. Visitors are advised that these concerts are suitable for children from six years old.

https://www.concertgebouw.nl/en/concerts-tickets?event_date=2018-03-14

Bos Amsterdam

Bos Amsterdam ("Amsterdam Forest") is a fun excursion just outside the bustle of the city. Enjoy nature walking, taking a bicycle ride, making a picnic, rowing, swimming, or visiting the goats at the two cheese farms that reside there. For you transportation lovers, the Tram Museum in Amsterdam offers rides on their historic trams to Bos Amsterdam for minimal fare.

- **Great Description:** https://www.amsterdam.info/parks/amsterdamse-bos/
- **Tram Museum:** https://www.museumtramlijn.org/EN/tramrides.php
- **Amsterdam Bos:** http://www.amsterdamsebos.nl/english/

The Tulips at Keukenhof Garden 2018

A bike tour to witness the tulips. The tulip season generally runs mid-March to mid-May. https://www.iamsterdam.com/en/see-and-do/things-to-do/activities-and-excursions/overview/veritas-visit-bike-tour-tulip-fields-keukenhof-area

A Day Trip to Edam

Wednesday is a great day to visit Edam's traditional cheese market. It's also a beautiful town. It's a half-hour drive (bus) from Amsterdam. Farmers bring their cheese to market loaded on boats or horse. This trip could also be a biking to tour.
https://www.ricksteves.com/watch-read-listen/read/articles/going-dutch-on-a-day-trip-from-amsterdam

Simply Awesome Trips
Itineraries Ready To Go!

A Day Trip to Kasteel de Haar in Ultrecht

This castle and grounds near Ultrecht look like a fun day.
http://www.dutchdutchgoose.com/2015/10/19/kasteel-de-haar-with-kids/
https://www.kasteeldehaar.nl/

A Day Trip to Alkamaar

Alkmaar is known for its Friday cheese market and takes 40 mins by train from Amsterdam. It could easily be combined with a trip to the windmills at Zaanse Schans. In Alkmaar, visit the Beatles Museum, Cheese Museum, Beer Museum, take a canal ride, and visit their historic church. https://grotekerk-alkmaar.nl/
https://www.tripsavvy.com/day-trip-to-alkmaar-1456658
https://www.kaasmuseum.nl/en/
http://www.beatlesmuseum.nl/info-eng/
http://www.biermuseum.nl/en/

See A Soccer Game

Amsterdam's football (soccer) team is Ajax Amsterdam, one of the most successful European teams in history. Watching a match at the local pub or the arena would be a great way to live like a local!
http://www.amsterdamarena.nl/

Happy Trails!

If you have an awesome photo and send it to us, #simplyawesometrips, we will post it to our instagram page. We love seeing your vacation photos. Honestly.

Non-liability Statement

Although the author has made every effort to ensure that the information in this itinerary was correct at the time of publishing, the author does not assume and hereby disclaim any liability to any party for any loss, damage, or disruption caused by errors or omissions, whether such errors or omissions result from negligence, accident, or any other cause. The authors, publishers, and contributors to this itinerary, either directly or indirectly, disclaim any liability for injuries, accidents, and damages, whatsoever that may occur to those using this guide. You are responsible for your health and safety for all aspects of this itinerary. Be safe and use good judgment.

By providing links to other sites, Simply Awesome Trips, does not guarantee, approve, or endorse the information or products available on these sites.

All maps courtesy of OpenStreetMap contributors www.openstreetmap.org/copyright

You Might Also Be Interested In:

Paris With Kids **by Simply Awesome Trips**

Athens, Greece **by Simply Awesome Trips**

Titles also available on www.simplyawesometrips.com and Amazon.com.

Made in the USA
San Bernardino, CA
16 July 2018